GW01045609

elite **St** *Street*

*The Elite Model Look: A Fashion and
Style Manual* ■ *Huggy Ragnarsson*

Virgin Publishing in association with Elite Special Projects

First published in Great Britain in 1998 by VIRGIN
BOOKS, an imprint of Virgin Publishing Ltd.
Thames Wharf Studios
Rainville Road
London W6 9HT

Published in the USA by Universe Publishing, a
Division of Rizzoli International Publications, Inc.
ISBN: 1 85227 797 1
Printed and Bound in Great Britain

Street*look*

"*The Street? I love it. Everything original and unique begins at ground level. It's about breaking all the rules and trashing the conventions. The heart and soul of art, music, attitude, and life itself are found on the street. And as any designer will tell you, fashion is born there. Open your eyes to the vibe and have the confidence to make your own choices; live your own life; believe you are special.*" Linda Evangelista

Click into interactive style with The Street, a now

This book is a slice of life, it shows you where you are and

the superhighway of fashion. It's not about what you wear,

Double-click on confidence because if you feel good, you

Live a little but care a lot. And keep your ear to the ground.

check the choices, learn the lessons the fun way.

Fashion

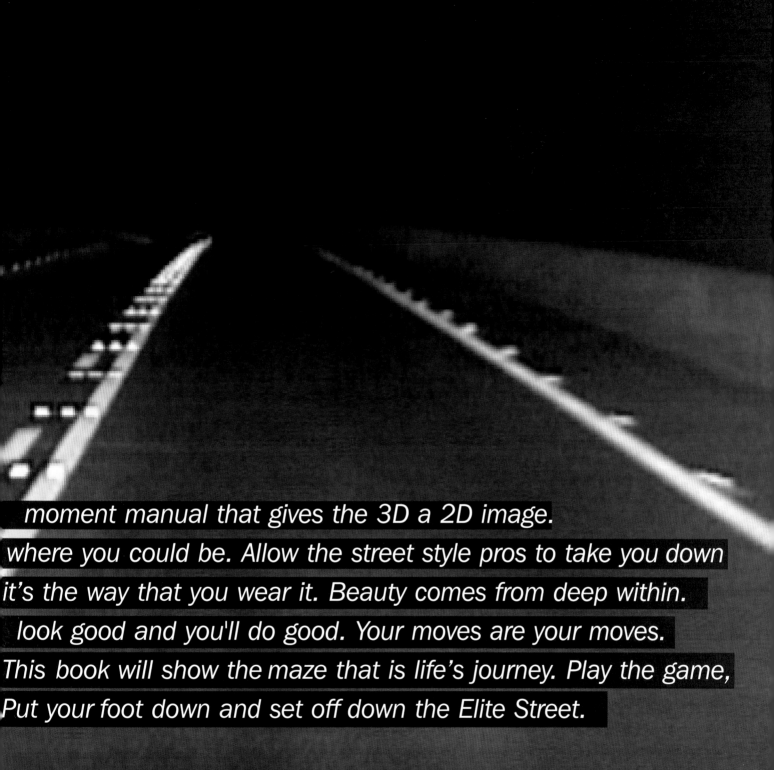

moment manual that gives the 3D a 2D image.

where you could be. Allow the street style pros to take you down

it's the way that you wear it. Beauty comes from deep within.

look good and you'll do good. Your moves are your moves.

This book will show the maze that is life's journey. Play the game,

Put your foot down and set off down the Elite Street.

Highway

Conte

*John***Casablancas**

Yfke *1997 Elite Model Look Winner*

Made in the Elite Street

The world of Elite Models focuses on life: always moving, changing, developing. With this book, we can bring great style and fashion as near as possible to our girls, our friends, and our clients around the world. The street is the nursery for much of this. We always look to the street.

*Gerald***Marie**

It's the street . . .

"I see pretty faces every day. Beauty is not just something you're born with—you have to earn it. Learning to love yourself, care for your body, and find inner peace is where you should be at.

"Once you know yourself, the search for style is clear and simple. You'll find it on the street. The street is speed, instant answers, and quick-fire sound bites for those who only have three seconds to surf."

Carole White *modelagent*
cwhite@elitepremier.com

Streetscene

Get sharp Rely on your own judgment and know your own mind. What suits you? Put some time and effort into finding out. You look great—with confidence you can pull anything off.

Your body Face up to the imperfections. Once you know where they are, you can minimize them. But be positive. What you consider to be a liability, someone else could be gagging for.

Your colors Forget what's "in." Hot pink isn't going to suit everyone (or anyone?). Find a core of neutrals—grey, black, navy, cream, and white—and offset them with accent colors. And then chuck all those ancient color rules out the window. Wear whatever color combination you feel great about.

Your style Fashion manuals will cast you in a type: classic, sporty, "trendsetter." Forget about it. Be comfortable, be practical, be appropriate—whatever that means to you.

Sharp strides Once you've bought into a look, try it out a few times at home. Make sure it's you. Happy? Go for it.

Get real Get yourself ready for real life. Take a look at the city life, summer life, day life, and nightlife on the street.   ***Debbie Bee***

FASHION SU S

Stop, take a look at yourself. What do you see, what do others see,

What's real?

Check out your look. Is it working? If not . . .

Can you make peace with imperfection?

The four models you'll be introduced to on these pages—Caroline, Tina, Ceri, and Amy—represent any girl, trying to assess for herself what is real and what is not. Getting to know yourself on the inside can get you rewards on the outside.

City_City_
Urban Street Warrior

City survival: _Do the trends, chase the scene, prepare for the future, protect yourself, be confident, give the right impression, don't be taken advantage of, find your different looks—if they work, stand fast!_

Urban Cowgirl

"The city was the bright light on a wide and empty horizon. When I was a kid, I used to watch movies and imagine that it was me catching the Greyhound heading for fame and fortune. Don't get me wrong, my hometown is no dead-end dump. I had so much fun, riding horses and stuff like that, meeting up with my schoolfriends and catching a movie. But once I'd graduated I couldn't wait to give the city a try. It was hard at first—I couldn't get used to seeing so many people at once and the noise of the city at night. I think my accent put people off a bit, too. I think they thought I was from nowhere but now I make it a talking point. They ask where I'm from and I start talking about Virginia and how different life is there. I love my life here now but part of loving it is the fact that I can go back any time. One day it may be for good.

"It's important to remember that in the midst of the pressure of the city, you can hold your own. Be proud of your background. After all, where you come from is who you are. It is what gives you an individual and unique sense of style."

caroline

The street is full of victims.
They blame anyone but themselves for what fate has thrown at them. But this life doesn't have to happen to you. You hold the cards - you make the choices. Street survival is a pro-active game. Live it and love it.

Street instructions

Arm yourself for the city. Prep your day, back up your attitude with thought while you walk. Don't leave home without:

● A diary with contact names and numbers of your appointments. Make sure you call if you are going to be late.
● A wallet/purse kept in a secure pocket.
● A makeup bag. Take advantage of freebie mini samplers from the cosmetic counter to lighten your load.
● A subway/underground map and a local guidebook. Get to know your way.
● A good book or magazine. Make the most of your free time.
● A Disc Man. Jive your day away.
● A snack in case of emergencies.

Street attitude

Rake
take and bake

The total you—polished and refined, with plenty of time. But looking this good takes preparation. You owe it to yourself to care for your body. Sounds like you need a top-to-toe overhaul. For total luxury, book a day of cool treatments at your nearest health club or take a weekend off for a beauty binge.

Find your direction for the next step of the game: the city. Define your elements, your character, and what you would like to experience in the world of style on the street . . . **THE SISTERS ARE IN THE HOUSE!**

polished

with plenty of time

Here's the checklist:

A Hair pack. Check out the moisturizing cream baths for hair which bump up the moisture content in the shaft of the hair after a couple of hours under wraps (particularly good after sunbathing).

B A peel or rinse-away face pack followed by a cooling, light moisturiser.

C Eyebrow reshape. Time to get rid of all those stray hairs.

D Eyelash tint. The most natural look for longer lashes.

E Body scrub. Look for one that contains seaweed to boost moisture content.

F Cream away excess hair, making sure that the skin is really clean before application.

G Manicure/pedicure. Give your nails a rest from polish. Work in some extra-rich nourishing hand cream to strengthen nails and prevent flaking and breaking.

H A full body, hour long, invigorating massage. This one you'll need help with. Tell your partner it is vital to complete your beauty regime (well, you can try).

ready for the

step of the game

ready for anything

top-to-toe care, top-to
Make grace, integrity,

Respect your body and relax your mind. Confidence comes from within but you've got to take care of the "without." Reach out. Learn to smile. Listen to your feelings. Laugh at yourself.

-toe confidence
and self-esteem work for you

Skin Police

Strip-search your skin right down to the pores. Total skincare

I skin types, to serve and protect you everywhere.

Basic skincare

The class-A skin criminal sleeps in a face full of cosmetics after a face load of excess. An unhealthy lifestyle makes for a dull skin tone and signs of premature aging. Even the wildest party animals tame up in time for bed. Give your skin the break it deserves. Adopt a routine that is fail-safe. Tattoo "cleanse, tone, and moisturize" onto your brain and don't forget a weekly gentle scrub to slough off dead skin. Take care now and get the payback later. Give yourself time off for good behavior.

The skincare criminals come clean

Want to know what yo
skin would look like if i
hadn't been exposed t
sun, city, and systema
abuse? Check out you
derriere. Although the
layers are thicker here,
your skin could be tha
soft, smooth, and clea
The skin is the biggest
giveaway on how you
your life. Insufficient sle

About face
The A to Z of total skincare

Adopt a beauty routine NOW.

Buy into baby softness. The beauty counter is stacked up with hypo-allergenic products for baby skins. Save your money, save your skin.

Cut out the crap. Fast foods containing chemicals and additives are total bad news.

Drink more water.

Eat healthily. Five portions of fresh fruit or vegetables a day is the way to keep skin clear.

Fake it if you have to. A real suntan is sooo uncool.

Greasy skin is a no-no. Choose oil-free moisturizers.

Holey cow. The dead giveaway of poor skin condition is enlarged pores. Watch out.

Irritated skin needs a break. Don't conceal it with makeup unless you really have to.

Just stop worrying. Stress takes its toll on skin just as much as a poor diet.

Kiss a lot. It's not good for your skin, but hey, it's fun.

Laughing causes wrinkles, but you're just going to have to live with a few.

Moisturize like it's going out of fashion.

Never use scented soaps on the face.

Oh no—spots. Make sure you don't irritate them.

Perfumed products may cause irritation. Check out the simplest creams with the most natural ingredients.

Quit eating junk food. It poisons your skin.

Repetitive actions, such as inhaling on a cigarette, cause premature aging. Believe it.

Soap-free cleansers leave more moisture in the skin.

The T-Zone hot spot that's across your forehead and down the bridge of your nose is where most grease is found. Try using a lighter moisturizer in this area.

Under-eye puffiness will disappear after a fifteen-minute soak under cooled cotton/wool pads. The tea-bag trick works but turns your eyelids brown.

Vitamin supplements are a quick-fix solution, but the most nutritious way to get healthy skin is to eat the right foods containing the vitamins and minerals you need.

Whip up a smoothie using raw vegetables and fruits. Your skin will love you for it.

eXfoliate—but go easy on yourself. Once a week with a gentle scrub is quite enough.

Yawning actions and facial exercises look pretty stupid in the mirror but they may well prevent those cheeks from sagging and that chin from doubling up later on.

Zzzzzzzzzzzzzzzzz—get some.

gs, cigarettes, and
ohol; stress; and
healthy eating will result
pimples, dark circles, dry
tches, greasy areas,
low tones, and telltale
nkles. Wake up to a
ole new skincare
tine. Check out the
mplete street A to Z for
ncare criminals
erywhere.

City heat

Pollution—what's your solution? Total body and hair care for maximum protection against the sun.

Before hitting the streets of the city, you need total-body protection. Pollution does its worst in the heat, and the sun is just as damaging away from the beach. The cumulative effect of daily doses of UV rays is prematurely aged skin. So make sure you wear an anti-UV day cream under your base foundation every day. The only lines worth having are the ones you get from laughing.

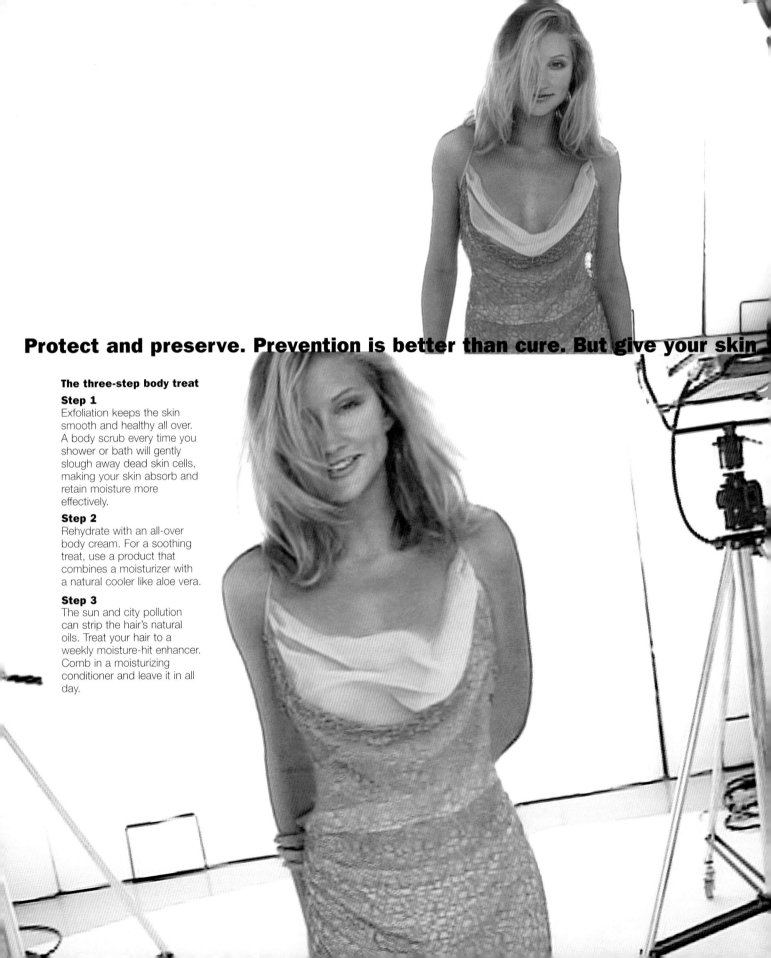

Protect and preserve. Prevention is better than cure. But give your skin

The three-step body treat

Step 1
Exfoliation keeps the skin smooth and healthy all over. A body scrub every time you shower or bath will gently slough away dead skin cells, making your skin absorb and retain moisture more effectively.

Step 2
Rehydrate with an all-over body cream. For a soothing treat, use a product that combines a moisturizer with a natural cooler like aloe vera.

Step 3
The sun and city pollution can strip the hair's natural oils. Treat your hair to a weekly moisture-hit enhancer. Comb in a moisturizing conditioner and leave it in all day.

and hair a weekly treat—a thorough cleanse and super moisturizing.

Go for the glow

Everybody looks better with a healthy skin color. Check out the latest

For a cool, sun-kissed look:

1 Choose a quality brand—one that specializes in skincare products.

2 Read the instructions carefully. Each brand has different requirements.

3 Test a little first. Try a small patch on your arm to make sure your skin is not sensitive to the brand.

4 Exfoliate very gently before application so that all the dead skin cells are removed and your skin is clear for coverage.

5 Go easy on knees and elbows. The cream may collect in the wrinkles and cause staining.

6 To avoid smears, apply quickly but carefully, making sure the spread is even.

7 Set your watch, take the phone off the hook, bolt the front door, and do nothing for the duration of the tanning time. You don't want to turn carrot-colored.

fake tans. It's the quickest and safest way to go for the gl

NAOMI
CAMPBELL JEANS

Naomi travels constantly. But she never leaves home without:

1 Intense hydrating mask
2 Hydrating b5 gel
3 Oxygen serum
4 Honeycomb mask
5 Foot cream or oil spray
6 Lip seal with vitamin E
7 Face spray
8 Nail file
9 Scissors
10 Revitalizing eye mask
11 Antibacterial hand gel
12 Face cream
13 Eye drops
14 Mouthwash
15 Toothbrush/paste
16 Hairbrush
17 Q-Tips

Street wise sharp

"Fashion spreads are about ideas inspired by a mood. Personally, I wear whatever I want to. But some people open a magazine and think, 'God, I've got to look like that.' That's when it's like, wait a minute. You look at it to get ideas, not to starve yourself and get anorexic."

Naomi Campbell

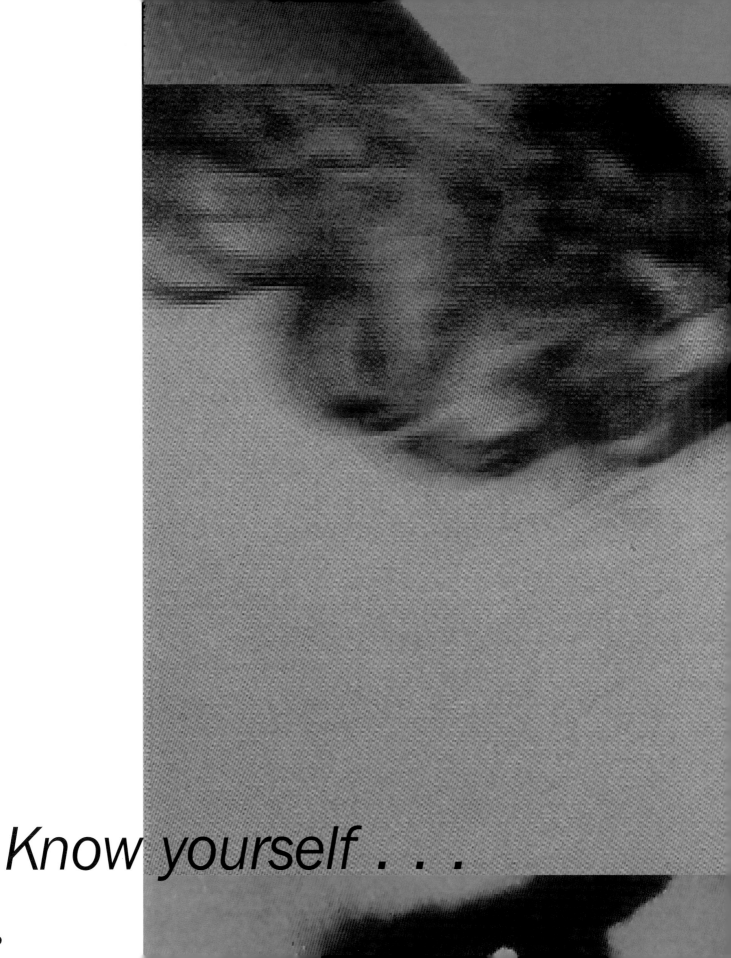

Know yourself . . . .

Invisible *See and not be seen*

Cool protection. It's essential to
Keep your eyes

Choose the shades that are right for you. The best shape contrasts the shape of your face. If you have a round face, choose square-shaped frames. If you have a long face, choose horizontal-shaped shades. Once you find the right shape, experiment with metal and plastic frames until you find some that suit your sense of style. Buy more than one pair for your changing moods. Just be sure they have adequate UVA/UVB protection.

elite*Models*Eyewear

have cool shades with UVA/UVB protection.
beautiful and keep yourself from being seen.

On the street, at the beach, in the country.

Pounding **the** *street*

Checklist for success

The natural you. Nothing to hide.

On meeting someone new, you have three seconds to make an impression. It's human nature to jump to conclusions. Make sure you're giving off the right vibe. Your body language gives everything away.

- **Walk tall** The way you hold yourself, even sitting, speaks volumes.
- **Stay cool** If you panic, you won't give your best.
- **Never bitch** If you have nothing good to say, don't say anything.
- **Eye to eye** If you can't meet a look, you will seem evasive.
- **Smile, go on** This could be your lucky break.
- **Prepare to personalize** You may have to talk about yourself. Choose topics that make you happy.
- **Listen up** And ask questions if you don't understand.
- **Be an early bird** Showing up late or flustered won't impress.

Give it your best shot

VOGUE HOUSE

External cooling system

Body *language*

Whatever profession you choose, you will have to handle a certain amount of rejection. Acknowledge and move on—you cannot be right for everyone because everyone is not right for you.

"Find out who you are and take charge of your life. Look after yourself and your family. Your roots are essential. Fight boredom and laziness; use your time well. You won't believe how happy life can be."

Be confident, be in control

KAREN MULDER

Timeout

Time out with

She's a star. Let her have her moment. Watch her shine and share the magic light. She will do the same for you when your time

friends is crucial. Time out for yourself is vital.

Learn to laugh at yourself instead of at others.

Be there when your friends need you.

Take sole responsibility for your actions.

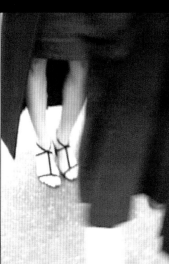

comes. Believe the impossible can happen and it will. Be strong for each other and keep your feet firmly planted on solid ground.

Overwhelmed?

Your life is incredible. The fact that you live and breathe is a miracle. You are one of the lucky ones. Even if your personal history has not been so easy, look on the negative points with a positive view. Take your experiences and help ease the problems of others. Give a little kindness back. Your community needs you.

Elite Models on a fitness run in Nice

When everything seems to overlap—
your work, your friends, the traffic,
the attitude—escape with body and
fly with mind. Change the range: be
polite and well-mannered, smile, be
kind and sincere, and cut the crap.
Serve the community best—
volunteer, teach, and show respect.

summer
life

Summer girl: *Sand castles on the beach, picnics, weekends away, warm days, cool nights. Get in touch with your natural energy, eat right, exercise, have fun in the sun but take care of your skin, make your own destiny, be an early riser, wash up, take the dog for a walk, smell the fresh air, pick up litter, ignore negativity, applaud creativity, do it all in style and . . . cut yourself some slack.*

Summer Dish: *"Any change of scenery is good, but if you are stuck in the city, you need to take time off and get outside. When I need a break from the heat, noise, and pressure of the city, I go to the beach to have fun and chill. It's the perfect place to revive and rejuvenate by relaxing in the sun, eating right, and getting some exercise.*
"When the weather is warm, it's a great time to get away. You need to follow the sun."

Tina

Get in touch with

Day*Star*

NATURAL ENERGY *Find the ultimate source*

Get out of the city, get out of your mind, get some natural energy, and find yourself energized. Time out on the beach is quality time for the soul. Get a life, and don't settle for anything less than the best.

Play

Pure

Power

The secret of eternal youth is never to grow old. But don't rely on a pot of moisturizer, search inside yourself. Find the child within. Make playtime a valid part of your daily life. Running, jumping, laughing, and having fun sound like child's play but they feed your soul and give you the energy to cope with the tough parts in life. Work, friendships, and relationships will fare better with positive power.

You heard it all in biology class but did any of it really seem relevant to you? Living off thin air may seem like a great way to shed pounds but actually you are doing far more harm than you can imagine. Your body is a finely tuned machine. Even if you can survive day to day on very little, the damage you are doing now may cause serious illness later on. Invest in your future, and you'll find that by eating a more nutritious diet, your metabolism will deal with excess pounds naturally.

Energize

Exercise

Five-minute skin survival

Minute 1
Remove all traces of makeup with a non-oily cleanser.

Minute 2
Exfoliate with a gently abrasive scrub to slough off dead skin.

Minute 3
With a toning lotion, pay careful attention to greasy areas, particularly around the nose, chin, and forehead, and in the hairline.

Minute 4
Moisturize all over, but tissue-blot areas prone to greasiness.

Minute 5
Protect against the sun and city with an SPF cream.

the POSITIVE POWER within

You bake, you flake

Suncare

A smothering of oil followed by intense heat will result in french fries. Unless you want your skin to look brown and crispy, use adequate sun protection. Always cover your face and body with a sunscreen and reapply every two hours to ensure maximum protection. Dark to medium skins need a cream with SPF 15. Fairer skins should start with SPF 25. The newer oil-free lotions won't stain your clothes and the latest sprays are simple to apply. Don't forget to reapply after swimming or exercise if the screen isn't water- and sweatproof. Skin cancer is the bottom line. A dark tan is soooo uncool. For a healthy glow, stay in the shade or look cool in a hat.

Who would you rather be with? A really good-looking guy

Beach*hangout*

makes you laugh, and

The sun is high, the waves are crashing, the sand is golden . . . and so are the guys! The beach is heaven— at least it should be.

ho spends half his time checking his reflection in your shades and the other half checking his pecs? Or a guy who is the most fun,

is genuinely interested in YOU? If that's what you're looking for, what d'ya think he's looking for?

Lighten up. If he doesn't like you because your swimsuit looks bad or your legs look heavy, maybe he's not the guy for you.

Beach
Summertime fun
Remember how to play hide-and-seek, volleyball, football, Frisbee, jump the wave, tag? Remember how to surf, exercise, swim, run, or even walk?

Body *Stop*

"Give yourself a break. It's time for chilling out."
Svetlana

Your body is ONE MEAN MACHINE. But don't abuse it. Learn to CARE

Listen up. Hard as it may be to believe, your body clock is ticking. That all-day, all-night party routine will have its revenge, and it'll happen sooner than you think. It's time to take a break and rejuvenate. Pamper yourself with a warm bath and unwind in aromatic oils. Revitalize your skin with a full body rub and follow up with a gentle all-over moisturizer. Have a vitamin binge with a fresh-fruit overload and drink gallons of still, cool water. Wake up energized in body, mind, and soul.

OR YOURSELF. You need REST AND PLAY as much as you need food and sunlight. RELAX.

Fab not flab

The secret to a perfect figure is to stop comparing it to other people's. Each individual has an ideal weight and size that can usually be achieved through healthy eating and exercise. Dump the diet. Get outta the blues. Changing your point of view can change your life... Sound mind and singing soul—go for it.

You have a perfect weight and size. You just need to find it.

Diets don't work. Changing your eating habits does. The trick is not to be convinced by quick fixes and fads. For example, eating only grapefruits all day will help you lose weight but will also throw your body into starvation mode with a slowed metabolism that's low on energy. Eventually you will have to give in. If you educate yourself in nutrition you will know that your body requires certain vitamins, minerals, fibers, and fats in order for you to remain healthy. Find your perfect size and shape by following the Street rules:

1 Kick-start your metabolism with a decent breakfast. Your mother is right: it is the most important meal of the day and should contain fresh juice, a fiber-full cereal with lowfat milk, and a piece of fresh fruit.

2 Snack on fresh fruit and veggies all day, and if you become tired and light-headed, have a biscuit or cracker.

3 Lunch on salads. Avoid dressings and sauces. Have pasta or potatoes or bread, but steer clear of spreads. Finish up with more fruit.

4 Supper should happen before six. Any later and your body may not have time to digest it before you sleep.

5 Keep your meals free of fat and fries.

6 The fresher the better.

Fitness *junkie*

Get strong. Exercise is more
joint mobility, posture, and breathing. Have

The six-pack sensation
strengthens stomach muscles.
The abdominal curl crunch
is a gentle rolling movement
that works the whole of the
abdominal muscle. Hands
slide up the thighs as the
abdominals squeeze and the
shoulders rise off the floor.

Steps 1 & 2
Place the weight of your head
in your hands so that the neck
is as relaxed as possible
during the curl.

Step **1**

than muscle power—it improves your flexibility,
the confidence to walk tall.

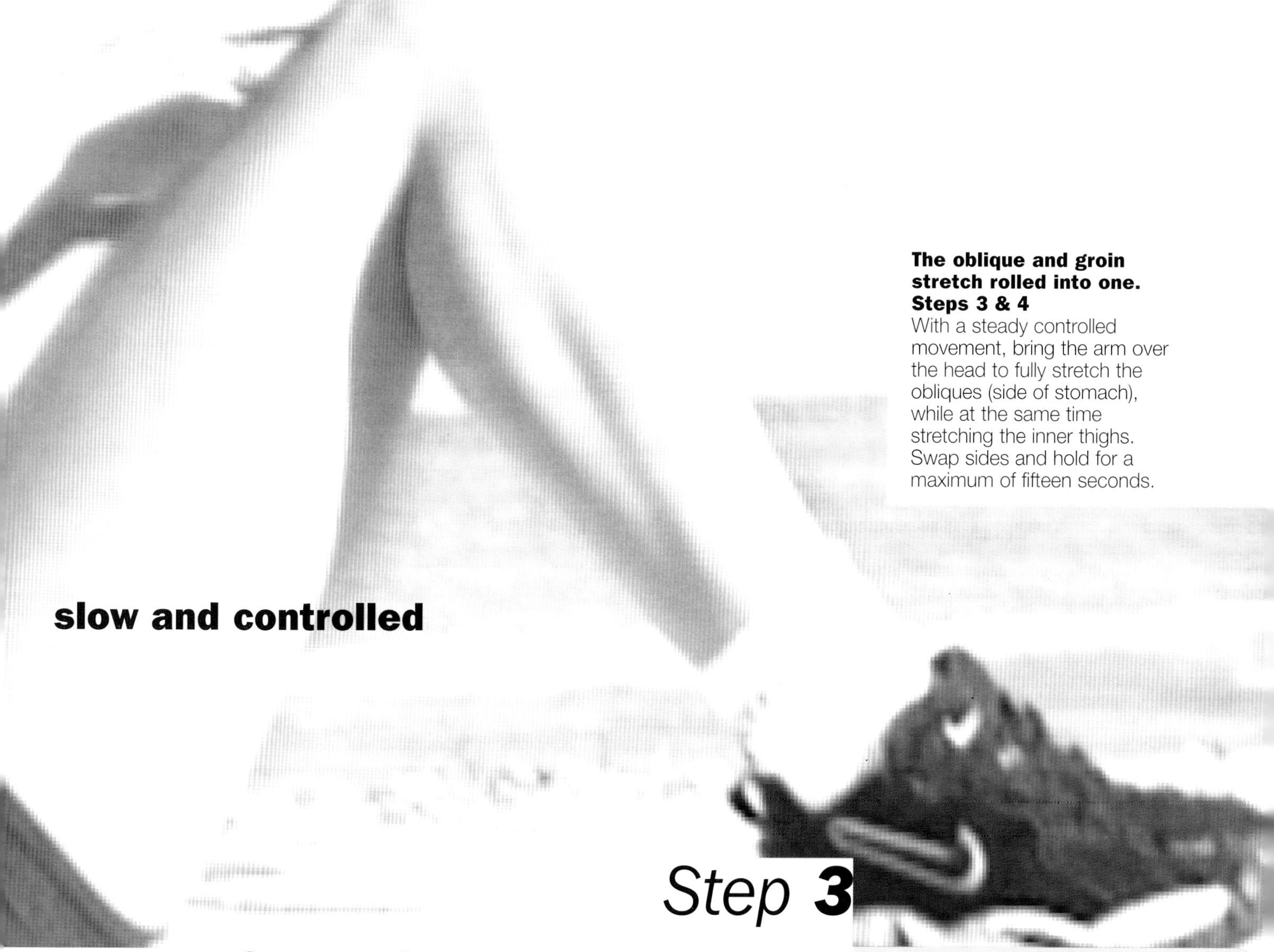

The oblique and groin stretch rolled into one. Steps 3 & 4

With a steady controlled movement, bring the arm over the head to fully stretch the obliques (side of stomach), while at the same time stretching the inner thighs. Swap sides and hold for a maximum of fifteen seconds.

slow and controlled

Step **3**

Step **2**

Step **4**

Step 1
Legs flat on the floor with arms extended over the head, palms upward.

Step 2
Bending slowly at the hips, reach toward the feet, stretching both lower back and back of legs. Keep it slow and take care not to overstretch. Hold for fifteen seconds.

Step 3
Ease off step 2 and resume step 1. Gradually increase the frequency of the stretching exercises. Breathe deeply and evenly throughout and try to clear your mind.

Step *1*

Stretch your body. Relax your mind.

Step 3

Stretch your body. Relax your mind. Stretch your body. Relax your mind.

Step 2

Strength toning exercise for the buttocks

Step 1
Place forearms on ground, with your head down. Keeping your head in alignment, straighten your leg so it is in line with your back.

Step 2
Bend your leg at the knee, while squeezing your buttocks to get maximum effect.

Step 3
Slowly lower leg at the hips to release contraction. Swap legs and slowly repeat the same motion.

Step 1

Step 1

Step 2

Step 3

Step **2**

Spine-mobilization and inner-thigh stretch

Step 1
Sit with your legs as wide as feels comfortable. Don't force it. Keeping your back straight, twist gently and slowly to the right side, stretching and mobilizing your spine and trunk. Make sure your head is facing toward the direction of the twist.

Step 2
Keeping the same position, twist gently and comfortably in the opposite direction and stretch the opposite muscles.

Step 3
Return to original position and repeat as necessary.

Heart workout

At the scientific end of the fitness business, the proof of the benefits of exercise are undeniable.

The cardiovascular workout machine

● Strengthens the heart
● Improves oxygen uptake from lungs into the blood
● Increases the number of oxygen-carrying cells
● Improves use of oxygen by the muscles

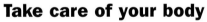

Take care of your body

Give your heart a workout. Spend at least twenty minutes three times a week running, biking, speedwalking, or doing aerobics. It's a great way to warm up your muscles before weight lifting and toning. Be sure to stretch thoroughly before and after.

tion

makes it tick? Listen to your heart. And go for it.

*Step **1***

*Step **2***

*Step **3***

At the correct intensity, exercise improves

Step 1

Step 2

your general fitness and burns up calories, a feel good factor ten.

Preacher curl
Upper-arm action for strength and muscle building.
Step 1
Place forearms, palms upward on the support pad. Grip curl bars firmly. Get comfortable.
Step 2
Keeping the elbows firmly on the support pad, flex the arm at the elbow. Ease the curl bar toward you.
Step 3
Continue the movement upward until the arms produce an angle just greater than 90 degrees. **Reverse the action and repeat.**

Leg Press
Work that butt off.
Step 1
Place feet flat on to the center of the push plate with knees at a 90 degree angle. Get comfortable.
Step 2
Ease legs out slowly but don't straighten them completely.
Now reverse the motion and repeat.

Limes

Give your hair some extra shine with a twist of lime in the final rinse.

Lemons

A squeeze of fresh lemon juice in tepid water makes a refreshing, zingy toner.
Also try cupping half a lemon on each elbow to break down tough skin.

Avocado For a nourishing facial dip, mush up half an avocado and add two teaspoons of fragrance-free moisturizer. Apply all over, avoiding the eye area. After five minutes, rinse thoroughly. Fend off anyone brandishing a tortilla chip.

Sun food

Endless cups of coffee or tea and cans of soda will only rob the body of valuable nutrients and put an even greater strain on the kidneys. The best possible source of water comes from fresh, raw vegetables and fruit. Keep caffeine drinks to a minimum and add four glasses of water to your daily intake.

Watermelon

Watermelon is one of the best sources of natural fluid and a refreshing way to cool down. And no calories.

Oranges

Fresh orange juice is the simplest way to get your vitamin C intake each day. But squeeze it yourself—the longer it stands, the less goodness it has left.

Papaya

Papaya contains vitamins and minerals that help protect the skin against the harmful rays of the sun. Great for breakfast, ice cold with squeezed lime.

ALOE

Aloe vera provides a soothing gel for sun-kissed skin.

SHOCK OF ARRIVAL

deal with confidence; approach life head on.
look it straight in the eye balance it out and welcome it with

Street survival
Don't be a victim. Don't accept what fate throws at you. Life doesn't happen to you—you hold the cards, you make the choices. Deal with confidence and meet the obstacles in your path head on. Street survival is a proactive game. Live it and love it.

open arms.

Leave the creep in

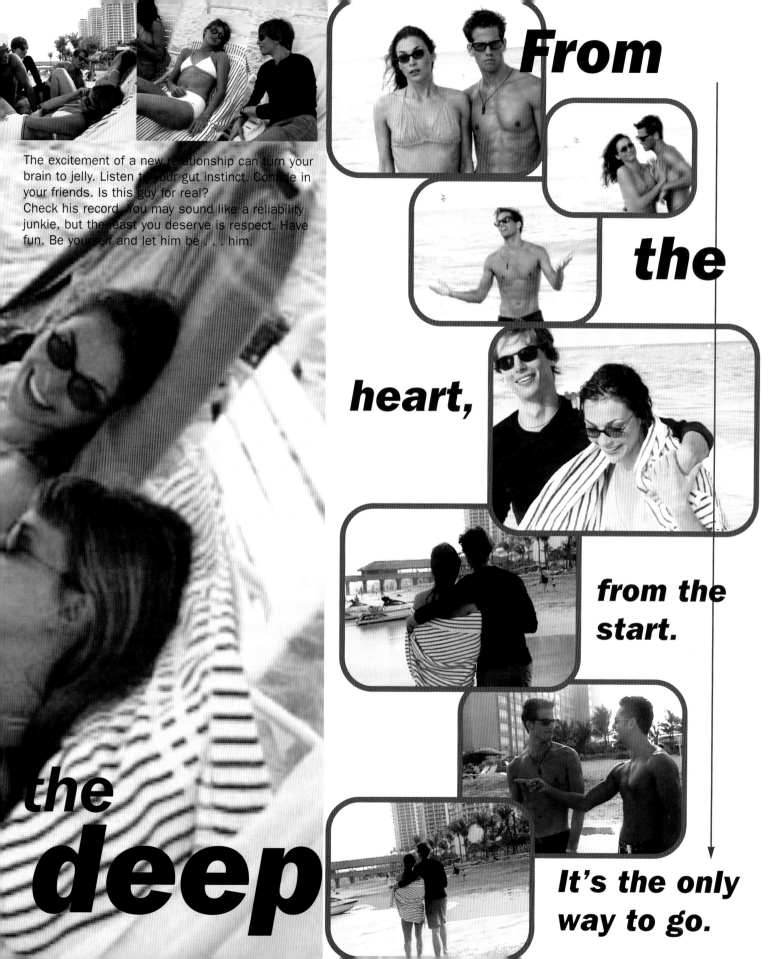

The excitement of a new relationship can turn your brain to jelly. Listen to your gut instinct. Confide in your friends. Is this guy for real?
Check his record. You may sound like a reliability junkie, but the least you deserve is respect. Have fun. Be yourself and let him be . . . him.

From the heart, from the start.

the deep

It's the only way to go.

"sure...

really"

The big "kiss off"

"When I first became a model, I was young, naive, and spoke very little English. I sometimes found myself in situations that were hard to handle. Language complicates it even more. Now that I speak English, it's easy, but before, if I wanted to deal with complete creeps giving me the come-on, I used two words—'really' and 'sure'—and then the other two words that everyone understands. Let me explain. He says, 'You're a very beautiful woman' and you say, 'Really.' He says, 'I'm totally in love with you' and you say, 'Sure.' He says, 'I can introduce you to Vogue.' Be upfront, respectful, honest, and direct, but if this doesn't work, you say, 'Kiss off' in the coolest possible way. Never be afraid to give a slimeball the big kiss off. Stay in control. Learn street English." *TERESA*

Night*life*

Night owl, night moves: *Peer pressure, true confessions, social slam. Organize your time, make the scene, keep a steady pace, stick to your guns, take advantage, don't be taken advantage of, watch your mileage and your night vision.*

"Although we covered topics at school on the dangers of drugs, alcohol, and smoking, I didn't know what the pressure would be like to join the 'in crowd.' If everyone else is doing stuff, you feel really dumb not joining in. When I first left home, I was totally naive. All these girls around me were taking stuff and staying out all night; they could never wake up and they looked terrible. I guess my background was really safe. Although I lived in a city, I had no serious contact with street life. You have to learn really fast. My parents don't have a clue what the scene is really like. I would never tell them—they'd be horrified—but I'm proud that I have worked out what is acceptable for me personally. There are some pretty tough choices out there." *ceri*

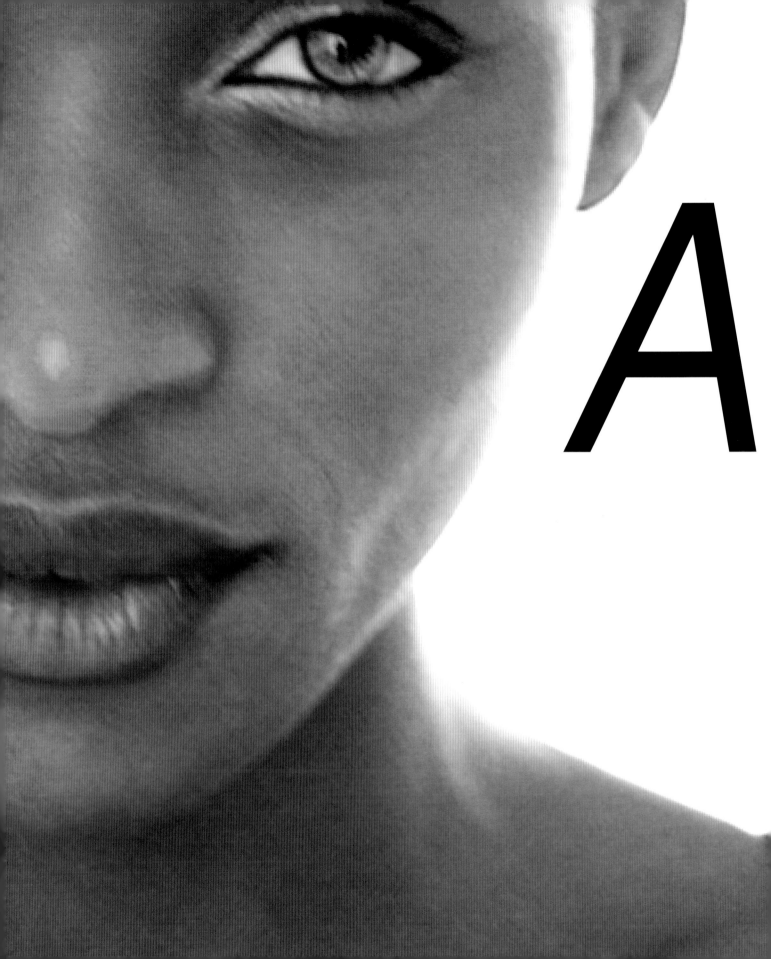

A

rtistic

License

Tool up. Fashion and beauty trends are constantly on the move. You need to be your own artist. Here are the top ten tools that no makeup artist's bag should be without:

1. Tweezers with shaped ends and a gripper bar will painlessly (well, nearly) remove stray brow hairs.

2. Lip salve—to save dry, cracked lips.

3. A light moisturizer—preferably oil free for emergency dry spots.

4. A toothbrush. A quick brushing between meals will brighten your smile.

5. Liquid foundation and sponge wedge—for a lightweight base to even out skin tones.

6. A translucent face powder—dusted lightly over to prevent high shine.

7. A natural lip color—to keep moisture in and lips well defined.

8. A waterproof mascara will add lush to lashes and a touch of color to brows if used sparingly

9. A neutral shade of shadow will add emphasis to eyes.

10. A concealer stick—just in case of a spot crisis.

Do you rate beauty over brains? Real people

Tender Loving Care, Tender Loving Care,

Artistic
License

Perfection or what? Imperfection or what? So what?

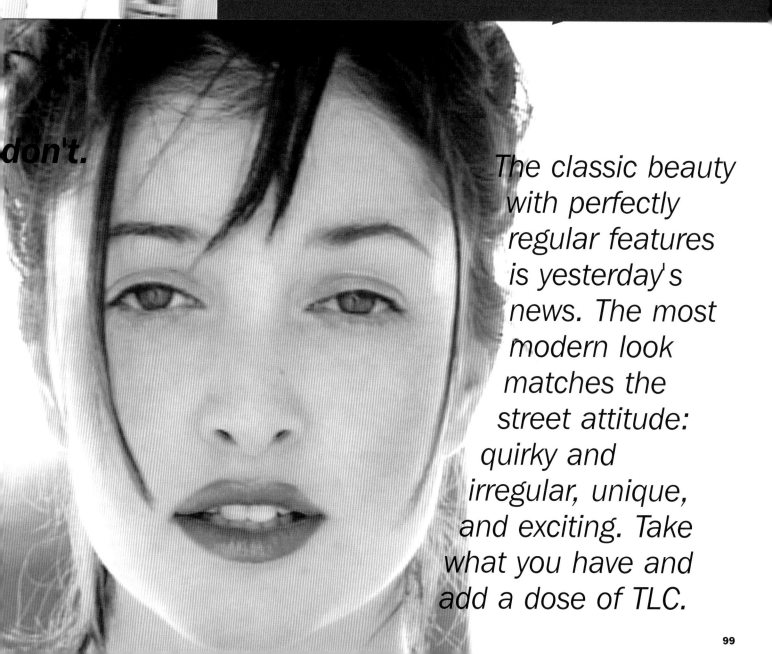

don't.

The classic beauty with perfectly regular features is yesterday's news. The most modern look matches the street attitude: quirky and irregular, unique, and exciting. Take what you have and add a dose of TLC.

face&eyes

Nights are for playing. Full-on face for maximum impact. Treat yourself to a professional makeover. Just one session will teach you how to make the most of your assets and identify your type. Your face is an empty canvas. Begin with a heavier base to even out skin imperfections. Set with a compact face powder. Shade and tone the eyes with stronger shades to balance the foundation. Double up on mascara, combing with a toothbrush between layers to keep the lashes separated. Use a blush to sculpt a bone structure, sticking to a skin tone shade a few tones darker than the skin color for maximum emphasis and minimum hot cheeks. Brush strokes from the hairline and don't overdo it. Line lips with a pencil to prevent smudging and fill in with a similar shade. Follow the color trends, but go with your instincts. And have fun; you don't have to take yourself too seriously.

War paint

"The street at night is the heartland of style and trend. Everywhere are new ways to think, new colors to see, and new products. Pay attention to different tastes, perceptions, and concepts. If it relates to you, try it." *AMBER VALLETTA*

Walk the walk

If you walked down the street like Naomi slithers down the catwalk, you'd soon be arrested. That walk is the smoothest, sexiest sidle ever seen on the runway. But what's crucial is that a walk can be learned and a shuffle can be unlearned. Hold your head high, thrust back your shoulders, and give it from the hip. Take up yoga or ballet if your posture is too ingrained. It makes a whole lot of difference to how you're perceived. Walk the walk. Walk tall.

"Whether you catwalk or faces and interesting bodies: up high; it's all about dignity, right, it makes you want to

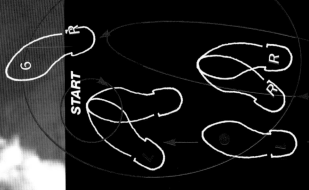

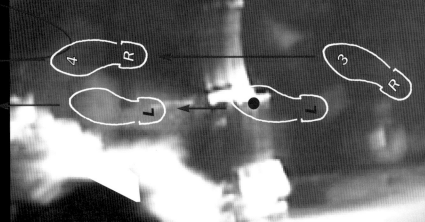

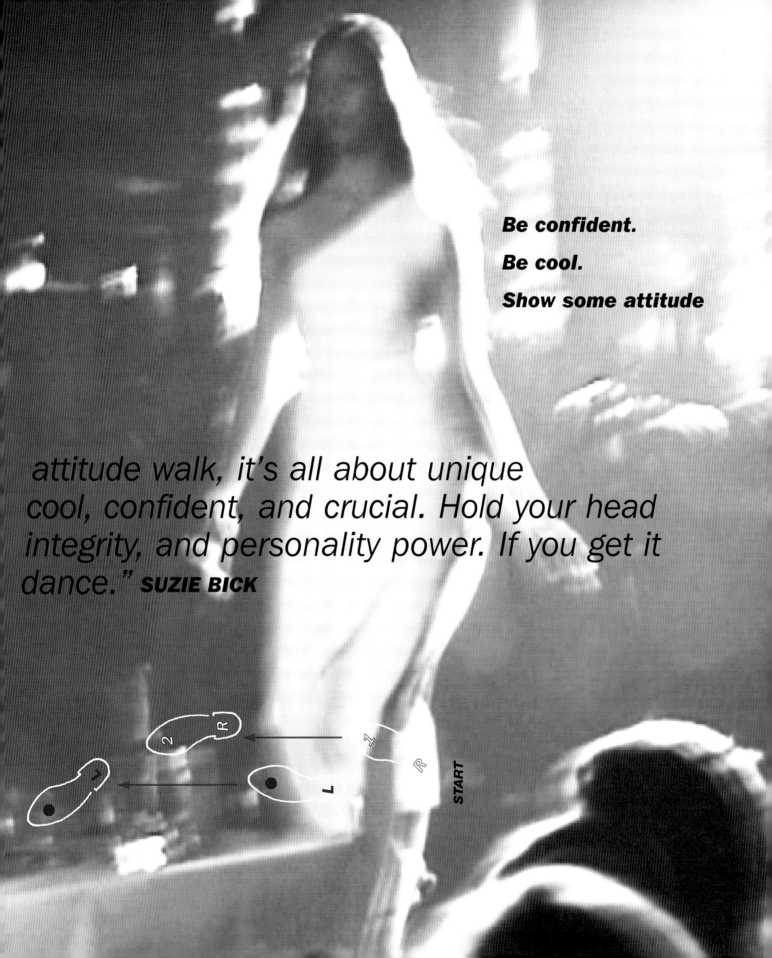

Be confident.

Be cool.

Show some attitude

attitude walk, it's all about unique
cool, confident, and crucial. Hold your head
integrity, and personality power. If you get it
dance." *SUZIE BICK*

"Lighten up or the street will blow you away" Lara Croft

Night *don't*

Alcohol, tobacco, and drugs. Don't

keeping up the habit.

crowd. If your friends are trying to persuade you, they're not friends.

The hardest people to say "no" to are your friends. Stick to what you believe. Make your choice but do so knowingly. If you need help, look to

t into any of them. Make sure you know the rules, the side effects, the cost to your body and soul, the expense of

s it really

worth it? Drugs won't make you part of the

They will rob you of your sense of self-worth.

friends outside your immediate circle or tell your family. Drug help lines are there for you too.

Cool water

If your fluid intake is less that two pints per day, you are not getting enough. If you are out
Water not only affects your internal organs, your kidneys in particular, it also affects

Have a healthy outlook on life. Enjoy it, live it, experience it, work at it, and love it.

clubbing, you should double that and add a few.
your skin.

No abuse, Only one life

Smoking sucks

Feeling great

Talk yourself out of it

is everything

The guide to street-smart quitting:

1 Make the decision to quit. To give up, you have to really want to. Don't do it for a partner or friend. Do it because you value your life and respect your body.

2 Take a shower, wash your hair, deep-cleanse your skin and put on fresh clothes. Now smell a smoker. Off-putting, huh?

3 Lose the evidence. Get rid of all the cigarettes and ashtrays from your environment.

4 Change your habits. If you smoke socially, try a change of scene. If you smoke at home, take up a new hobby—one that involves your hands.

5 Change your lifestyle. Swap a smoker's routine for a healthier regimen. Make use of your spare time in the gym.

6 Get fit. Smoking will wreck your health and fitness. Get down to the gym and spend your time caring for your body instead.

7 Dump the no-hopers—the friends who offer you cigarettes don't want to face their own addiction. Leave them alone until your stamina is stronger.

8 The most successful quitters give up entirely with no relapses—you can't afford them. Use nicotine alternatives, such as the patch, if you feel you need to.

Unique&Unlimited

Revive

A bad-head day. What kind of abuse did you put your body through last night? GET UP!

Choose a friend who is high on sympathy and low on "told-you-so's." The occasional blow-out helps define your limits and allows you to

out to detox. Binge out on fresh fruits and raw vegetables. Get some air

your body. What to do the morning after a night out.

Sorry, get up. Get your metabolism into first gear. Squeeze yourself an O.J., double it up with a glass of water, and have some breakfast.

get to know yourself through other people on the scene. Take a day

and some good advice. But make sure you

have a clear day ahead. Now is the time to begin

The street is life

"The street can seem tough, but don't be afraid of it. Observe your surroundings carefully and learn from them. Look at what's around you. Check out the style, culture, energy, and sites of the street. Be creative. Take from it what you want. Being street-smart will give you confidence. Before long, you'll feel like the street belongs to you."

Emma

Passion

Do not mist___ ____t for love. Recog___ __e importance __ __ste___g to your mind a_ __ell as listening to __ur heart. Take it slow. Mak_ _ure he's right for you befo__ moving __ the next step.

Sincere positive interest? Make sure.

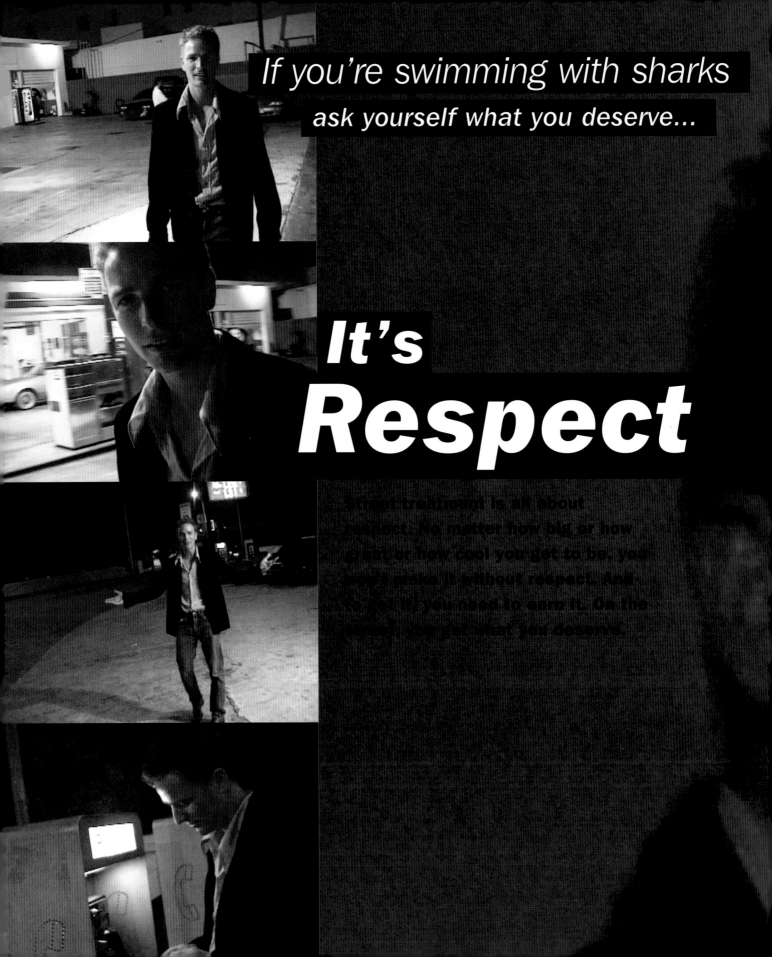

If you're swimming with sharks

ask yourself what you deserve...

It's
Respect

or reject

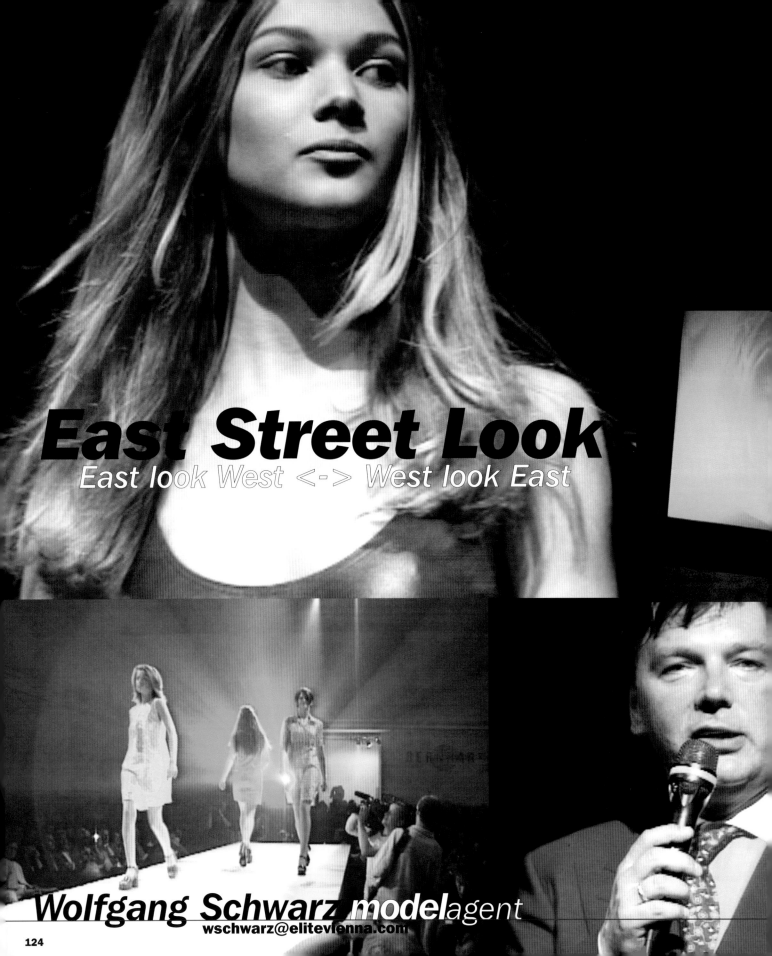

East Street Look
East look West <-> West look East

Wolfgang Schwarz modelagent
wschwarz@elitevienna.com

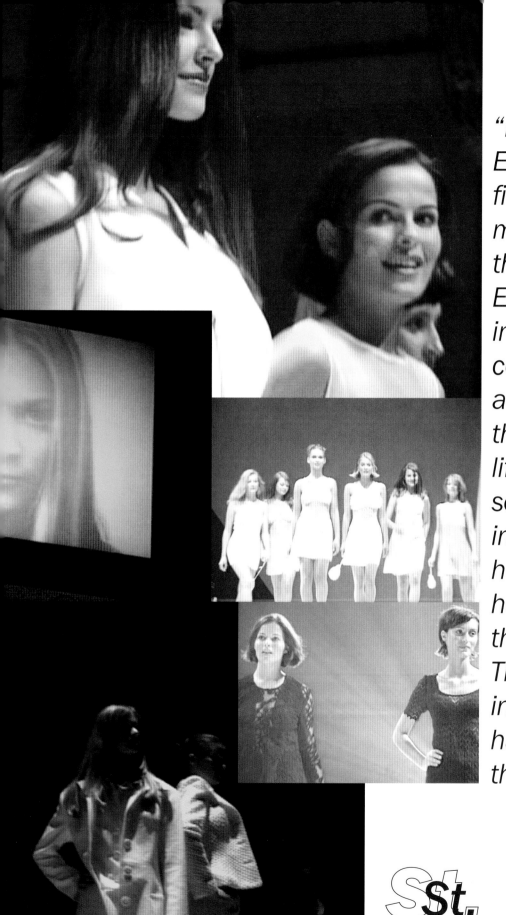

"I scout all over Eastern Europe to find some incredible models. Many of them need to learn English. The images, style, and cool from the street are a vital part of their education in life. They will learn self-respect and the importance of a healthy body, a healthy mind, and their independence. There is no real instant success; it has to be earned the hard way."

Daylife
Daygirl

Preparing for the pressure, organizing time, working the scene, making social connections, keeping a steady pace, watching your back, and checking your e-mail. Or escaping the race, taking a deep breath, exercising, eating well, framing your mind right for weekends and holidays, shopping, home comfort, relaxing, seizing the day.

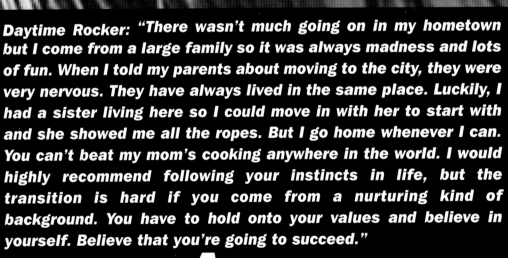

Daytime Rocker: *"There wasn't much going on in my hometown but I come from a large family so it was always madness and lots of fun. When I told my parents about moving to the city, they were very nervous. They have always lived in the same place. Luckily, I had a sister living here so I could move in with her to start with and she showed me all the ropes. But I go home whenever I can. You can't beat my mom's cooking anywhere in the world. I would highly recommend following your instincts in life, but the transition is hard if you come from a nurturing kind of background. You have to hold onto your values and believe in yourself. Believe that you're going to succeed."*

Amy

I feel alive I feel alive I'm fe

wide open spaces, *far away dreams*
      Enjoy the outdoors. Breathe in the fresh air. Allow yourself to relax.

live
n' good

Summer Look

Lazy summer hair and makeup

Keep it simple. Leave your styling tools at home—take only your UVA sunscreen. Go for the five-minute hairdo, not the five-hour one. Twist and sculpt hair into place. Secure it with clips that are meant to be seen. Let it down into "Titanic" curls for the night. Don't let your hair become damaged. Put a cap on or sunblock treatment. It can be left on all day to stop color fade and frizziness. Chlorine isn't washed out by normal shampoos. Read the labels. Don't end up with green or "Barbie" hair.

Get a grip. Summer hair should be simple and easy. If it takes more than five minutes to do, it's going to look too neat and fussy to look cool for the heat and humidity of long sunny days and evenings.

Summer hair should be done but undone, easy and not contrived.

Keep the cosmetic bag small!
Make sure you exfoliate at night.
Don't let the summer lag on your
skin. Put your UVA protection on
an hour before you hit the beach.
This is where to spend your money
so you don't end up looking like
one big brown spot. Avoid greasy
potions. Don't forget your lips.
Choose a lip balm with protection.
Take your moisturizer but leave the
powder at home. Gloss the skin
with your favorite spray.

A hairdo is really a hair-don't in summer.

dirty hair

Sharp shooters are out gunning for grease and grime. There's no excuse. Whatever your type, shade, or style, your hair can be your blazing glory.

Even over-processed hair can be given new shine and volume

. . . *MAKE MY DAY!!!*

Hair *solution techniques*

Simple hair solution techniques

First off, identify your hair type—70 percent of haircare problems are caused by the wrong product choices.

Overworked hair has been processed, colored, or semi-permanently curled. It will tend toward dryness and breakage, especially at the ends. Choose a deep-moisturizing shampoo and leave-in conditioner. Serum will prevent flyaway strands and frizz. Use after blowdrying for maximum control.

Pretty damned normal hair requires thorough cleansing to keep it that way, as well as a light hand with the conditioner. Don't be tempted to wash it too often; every other day is enough. A very small amount of serum used before blowdrying will add volume without making your hair look greasy.

Greaseball hair is easy to disguise. Choose a specialist shampoo and go easy on conditioner. Stick to a rinse-out type and apply where it is needed most—usually at the tips, which dry out first. Agitate the scalp as little as possible and use a styling brush when the hair is almost dry.

Shortcuts to a healthy head of hair

Expert help is always at hand. Find a stylist you can trust to give you practical advice that won't leave you shafted.

Change your shampoo regularly. Sticking to the same brand may leave your hair looking lackluster. Use a separate shampoo and conditioner and apply moisture only where your hair needs it.

Avoid heat damage by allowing hair to dry naturally whenever possible. A professional blow-dry should last twice as long as a home cook. Give yourself a treat.

Plan your treatments. A change in color or style needs careful consideration.

*Street*Moods

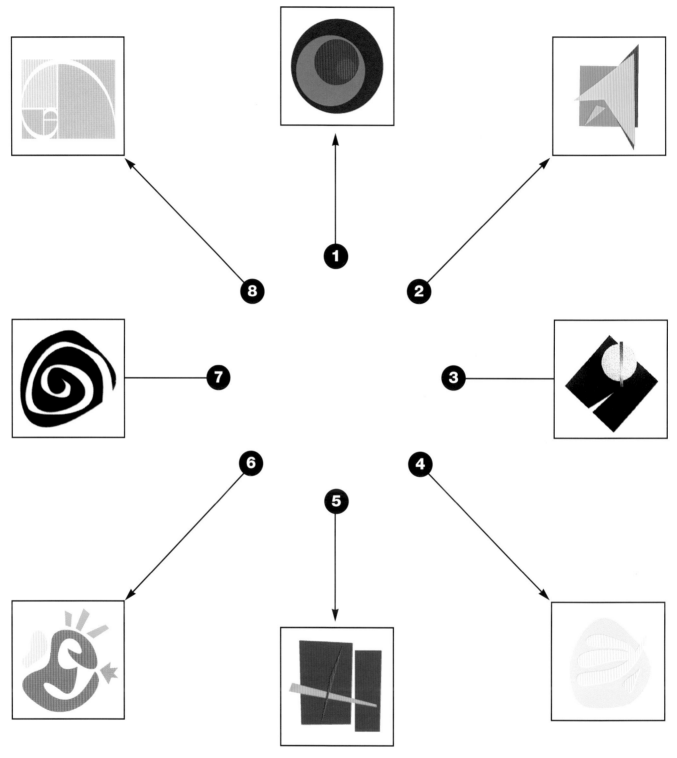

Instant mood discovery

Stop for a moment and take a look inside. Get in touch with your innermost feelings. Assess your moods—what makes you upset or angry? Try to gain insight into your emotional needs and discover ways to keep yourself well-balanced and in touch with your behavior. Next time you're at the computer or at a cyber cafe, you can try a detailed personal mood analysis for you and a significant other. Go to personal-test.com (checkup.de in Germany). Get to know more about your inner self.

"Our favorite colors reflect our mood and reveal our inner self. These colors also tell us which fragrance best expresses our personal style. Traditional color analysis places you into a standard personality type. Mood discovery provides an individualized analysis that can heighten awareness of your present emotional needs and give you a more intimate understanding of others. This simple mood discovery is fun and enlightening. Check it out."

Rosemary Fergurson

*Fashion*is*passion*

Forget the rules you learned about dressing for your body type, like not wearing horizontal stripes because they make you look too wide. Wear what you love. Anyone can find clothes to emphasize her special personality. What looks right and feels right is up to you. Find cosmopolitan combinations for your lifestyle with Elite Models' Fashion, day by day, every day.

Active - Gym - Daily Fashion - Flirt - Easywear

elite

Mall Maniacs - Get the look

BEFORE YOU HIT THE MALL

● Read up on the runways. The season's trends will be hitting the high streets but you need to think about which ones you want to buy into.

● Clear out your wardrobe. Separate the clothes into **a**/don't wants—take them to a charity shop, **b**/maybes—but they need an update, and **c**/old faves—understand why you look good and feel good in these. Make a mental note to buy into these again.

● Get real. Only buy what you need and what you can afford. Store/credit cards can stretch your budget but the debt may outlive the clothes. Shopping should be fun so set a budget and stick to it.

Have I missed something important?

Do I look good in this?

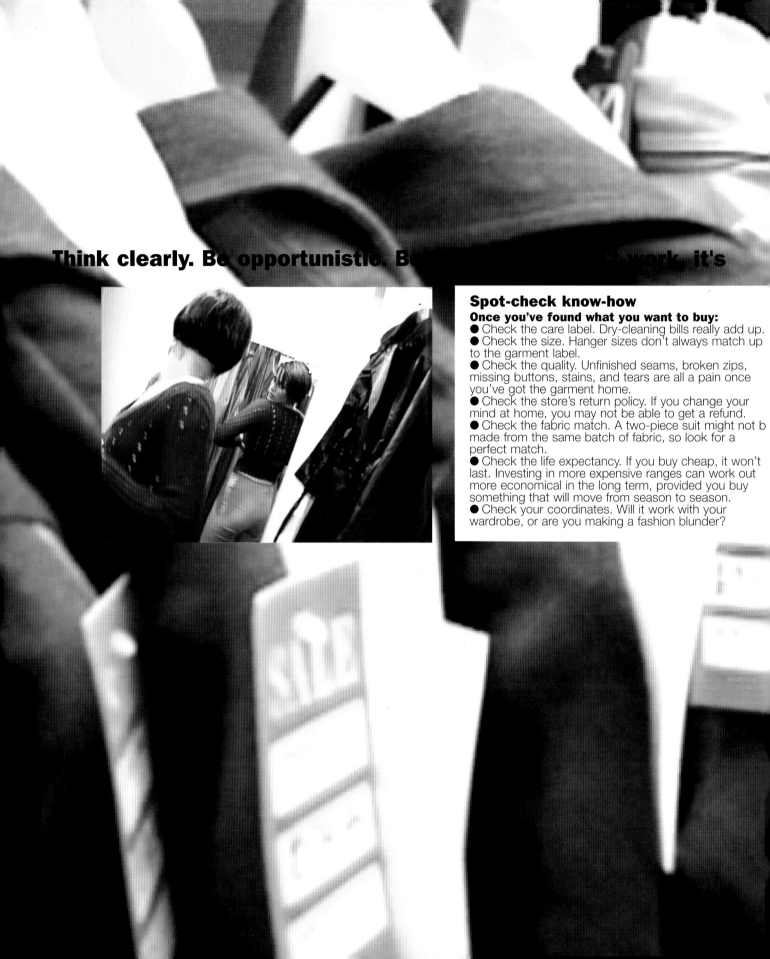

Think clearly. Be opportunistic. B   work, it's

Spot-check know-how
Once you've found what you want to buy:
● Check the care label. Dry-cleaning bills really add up.
● Check the size. Hanger sizes don't always match up to the garment label.
● Check the quality. Unfinished seams, broken zips, missing buttons, stains, and tears are all a pain once you've got the garment home.
● Check the store's return policy. If you change your mind at home, you may not be able to get a refund.
● Check the fabric match. A two-piece suit might not b made from the same batch of fabric, so look for a perfect match.
● Check the life expectancy. If you buy cheap, it won't last. Investing in more expensive ranges can work out more economical in the long term, provided you buy something that will move from season to season.
● Check your coordinates. Will it work with your wardrobe, or are you making a fashion blunder?

character building. But don't worry—you learn quickly.

Hush Hush Darling

Center yourself and chill

Learn to relax. Breathe before you speak and you can eat at stress's table. Use relaxation products, both natural and cosmetic. Stretch for excellence. Learn the five-minute rescue remedies and the top chilling music ever. Stay in touch with life by reading books, newspapers, and magazines. Paint, draw, write, sing, sew, **or whatever.**

Stress goes with any territory. Learning to switch off and take time out is vital. But everyone needs to find their own personal stress buster—it may be reading a book, swimming laps, or having a relaxing bath. Here's what the street pros recommend:

Linda: "I love music so much. When I'm totally exhausted after work there's nothing like listening in the candlelight." **Teresa:** "I guess I relax by going back to Prague. I am a patron of an orphanage back home and make sure that I visit at least every few months. Seeing those children really puts my problems into perspective. They are such a joy to be with." **Tina:** "Tai chi—I swear by it. I felt like an idiot at first, waving my arms around and stuff, but once you get over yourself, you really do feel more peaceful." **Ceri:** "I book into a spa for a day. There's a great little place in New York where you can get massages, skin treats, and all sorts of relaxing stuff. And they don't throw carrot juice and rice crackers at you the whole time. It's a luxury, but worth it."

Naomi: "I keep my bible by my bed—wherever I go, it goes with me." **Amy:** "As soon as things start getting to be too much, I go home to see my folks. There's nothing like some of mom's home cooking to sort my life out." **Caroline:** "I read. It's a great escape, especially when I have so much waiting around to do. And in between appointments, I can snatch a few pages."

Emma: "I've just discovered aromatherapy. At the Body Shop they can tell you which oil would work best for you. You can put together your own little potion and either burn it or put a few drops in your bath. Heaven." **Lara**: "I take to the highways on my bike—or hit the computer."

Look to the inspiration of the sky. Its endless beauty is unique like every sunrise and sunset.

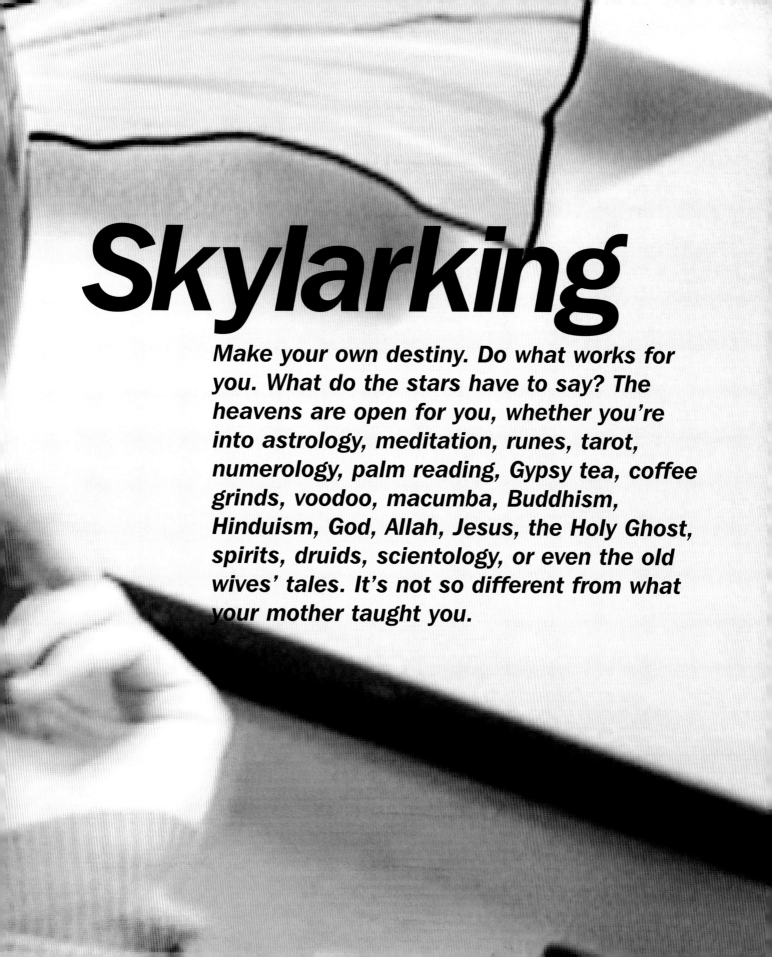

Skylarking

Make your own destiny. Do what works for you. What do the stars have to say? The heavens are open for you, whether you're into astrology, meditation, runes, tarot, numerology, palm reading, Gypsy tea, coffee grinds, voodoo, macumba, Buddhism, Hinduism, God, Allah, Jesus, the Holy Ghost, spirits, druids, scientology, or even the old wives' tales. It's not so different from what your mother taught you.

MindTime

Look for knowledge. Learn to type. Surf the net. Make the most of your down time. Sitting on a bus or waiting for an appointment offer free periods for your brain. Don't turn into a magazine junkie—get yourself some knowledge.

Super brain power
Here's what the girls do to keep their brains ticking:

Linda is mad about art deco. She reads up so that wherever she goes, she can check out the flea markets and antique shops. She's also an authority on cigars.

Naomi has recently become involved with Nelson Mandela and organizations in South Africa. Her involvement in charity work and world politics means she has to get into the history of every country that she visits.

Claudia is a language nut— she already speaks seven.

Christy and Amber are back in college.

Karen has a great voice and is taking lessons.

Opinions over attitude. Be calm. Be cool.

the internet - art & history - sports - cooking - the environment

Expand your mind

learn girl
smile girl

It's portable, it's practical, and everything you need to know can be found in it. What is it? A book. Choose a subject you have an interest in, anything at all. Once you have established what you want to learn about, check out courses at nearby colleges. If you are on the move, consider a correspondence course. It won't cost a fortune and you won't have to commit to anything to start with. But you should make a commitment to yourself. Expand your mind. What you're doing now won't last forever. You may want a change and if you start to learn today, you are investing in all your tomorrows.

dance - massage - aromatherapy - religion - movies - television - music

Sleeptodream

So it's totally cool to stay out 'till dawn, but at some point you'll have to catch up. Without eight hours of uninterrupted sleep each night, your work will get sloppy, your skin will turn sallow, and your attitude will suck. Make sleep a priority ritual.

Dreamy *sleep*

For maximum zzzz follow the five-step formula.

1 Eat early. Your digestive process slows right up when you are sleeping. A meal before bedtime will keep you awake.

2 Get the temperature right. Your body temperature drops by 1°F during sleep so snuggle into jammies.

3 Scent your pillow. A few drops of eucalyptus oil will keep you breathing regularly, even during a cold.

4 Stop worrying. Problems become insanely huge in the middle of the night.

5 Steer clear of buzz drinks before bedtime. Coffee, chocolate, and Coca-cola will have you crawling around the ceiling for hours. Try a chamomile tea instead.

Street is a way of life, a journey, and an incredible adventure. It first started for me at sixteen as a model and has taken me as a photographer through the streets and cities of the world. The photos and filming that you see here are not only a recollection of that journey but also a document of my vision, truth, philosophy, trends, people, and great friends.

London

Elite Premier Models: Amy Howsam Ceri Evans Caroline Farrington Emma Blocksage Lara Croft Linda Evangelista Claudia Schiffer Naomi Campbell Karen Mulder Amber Valletta Svetlana Teresa Maxova Tina Harlow Rosemary Fergurson Spela Sola Abdul Olivia Walmsley Kate Groombridge Iris Thorarinnsdottir Georgina Cooper Ingrid Seynhaeve Sophie Anderton **Elite Premier London:** Carol Gareth Sam Carly Abby Kirsty Jules Gary Dan Paul Debbie Miranda **Elite Model Look international:** Marie O'Niel **Apple Computer:** The Macintosh Desktop Publishing System **Human Interface:** Ian Sweet (The High Commander) **True Spirit Ltd:** Richard Stegmann **Supreme Motor Carriage Company:** Sean Tony **Metro Studios:** Special thanks to: Alan Strutt Ferny Chung **Tapestry:** Photographic Prints Paul and Terry **The Worx:** Lynn **Make-up:** H.B. **Hair** Donna Allen for **Smith's Salon** Also for the hair and make-up technique text in Wide Open Spaces and **A Very Special Thanks** to Vincent Smith **Stylists:** Alison Fitzpatrick Jason Leung and Jiv **Travel:** Paul at Strand Travel and Virgin Atlantic **Locations:** Vogue House The Bailey 32 Great Queen St. London Zilli Fish The Collonade Hotel, Warrington Crescent W9 **Housing and Hospitality:** Marie O'Neil and Olivier Castagne **Camera Eye Ltd:** The David Bailey "DB" camera, equipment and travel bag Collection. Glen Carron Cashmere

Miami:

Peggy Bremner Inc. Peggy Diane Eddie Marie-luce Kirk and Jeffery Julio Alex Carlos **Hair/make-up:** Chen ho Christine Reyna Jane Pittman **Stylist:** Lucy **Elite Miami Models:** Carolina **Elite Miami:** Capucine **Boss Models:** Miami Sarah Hamilton-Bailey Grabrielle Arter **Boss Models:** Lisa P Nealy Wim Jeff Bloom Arlynd Will Johnston **Equipment:** Dolly at Studio South Ford Expedition via Mike Abrams at Freindly Ford North Miami **Locations:** Lizzy Grubman PR and Shawn for Groove Jet Miami Sheldon's drugs and sundries Bal Harbour, Fl. Robar hair designers Surfside, Fl. Freddy at Sands Pointe Miami, Fl. and Roy Dacosta at **Premier Limousines**

EXTRA VERY SPECIAL THANKS FOR GREAT SUPPORT TO:

Chris Owen Jonathan Clayton - Jones Ian Sweet Debbie Bee Roger Richter Lisa Smith @ Mission Roger Eaton Claudia at Metro Tina Harlow Suzie Bick (Courtesy of IMG) Lara Croft (Courtesy of EIDOS) Linda Evangelista Claudia Schiffer Amber Valletta Naomi Campbell Theresa Maxova Svetlana Rosemary Fergurson Karen Mulder Carlton Gardner Trudi Tapscott Nancy Roberts at Marie Claire Carol White John Casablancas Gerald Marie Alain Kittler Pio Di Biase Wolfgang Schwarz Carlo Salvi Zane O'Donnell Marie O'Neil Michael Lu Priscilla Jerome Zagury Xavier Moreaux Guillaume Doret Pall Stefansson at Atlantic Review Reykjavik Kaya Eyfjore Asta at Eskimo Models Denni Karlsson Jon Helgasson Dr.Thorarinn Arnorsson's family Charles Miers Alex Tart Carmel Allen Dr Joachim Mensing at Moodform Charmaine Mensing and family Mark Steverson Harvey Tanton and Millie Mario Louis at Carmel Assocs Alan Ditton at Coutts and Co Ronnie Harris Peggy and Thio Olivia Owen Sissy Best and all at Northbourne Park School Clive Reed AFB Kay Brusaferro Hilmar Ragnarsson Carol Macdonald-Bell Trisha and Nigel Jonathan Pang Fashion Cafe Aldo Zilli Dr Fred Lim Sarah Ben and Harry The Covent Garden Hotel

P.S. Check out these WEB sites.... www.checkup.de   www.personal-test.com
elitepremier.com   elite.com   huggyragnarsson.com   amazon.com   virgin-books.com/people

All trademarks acknowledged.